Myth Quest
Uchchaishravas

THE DIVINE FLYING HORSE

retold by Anu Kumar

illustrations by Maya Magical Studios

First published in 2012 by Hachette India
(Registered name: Hachette Book Publishing India Pvt. Ltd)
An Hachette UK company
www.hachetteindia.com

SRD

Text copyright © 2012 Anu Kumar
Illustrations copyright © 2012 Hachette India

Anu Kumar asserts the moral right to be identified as the author of this work

All rights reserved. No part of the publication may be reproduced, stored in a retrieval system (including but not limited to computers, disks, external drives, electronic or digital devices, e-readers, websites), or transmitted in any form or by any means (including but not limited to cyclostyling, photocopying, docutech or other reprographic reproductions, mechanical, recording, electronic, digital versions) without the prior written permission of the publisher, nor be otherwise circulated in any form of binding or cover other than that in which it is published and without a similar condition being imposed on the subsequent purchaser.

ISBN 978-93-5009-323-8

Hachette Book Publishing India Pvt Ltd,
4th & 5th Floors, Corporate Centre;
Plot No. 94, Sector 44; Gurgaon 122003, India

Typeset in Adobe Garamond Pro 13/16
by Eleven Arts, New Delhi

Printed and bound in India by
Manipal Technologies Limited, Manipal

Welcome to the world of MythQuest . . .

Discover the fables and legends about the origin, history, deities, ancestors and heroes of India.

While the term 'myth' in common conversation means a false story, in the world of religion, folklore and magic, myths are considered 'true'. They tell stories of the creation of the universe, the eternal battle between good and evil and the history of humankind itself.

The main characters in our myths are bigger and better than any modern superheroes. They are birds and beasts, gods and demons, kings and queens, generals and warriors, sages and gurus, each with extraordinary powers that changed the course of history and the fate of the human race.

The people to whom a myth belongs consider it a true account of their past millions of years ago. Even today, they continue to worship the gods and goddesses, follow the rituals and read the texts that developed from these myths.

Hachette India's MythQuest series brings to you fascinating stories from the vast treasures of ancient mythology. Read them all—and become a MythMaster!

Mythological characters and events have been described in different ways in different versions of ancient texts. We have chosen the most interesting and key stories to build a comprehensive account for the young reader.

This story is about . . .

. . . Uchchaishravas, the magnificent celestial horse, who is said to be one of the divine creatures born of the churning of the divine Ocean of Milk.

This glorious seven-headed horse was the king of all horses and possessed exceptional powers. Not only could he gallop across the earth, he could also fly across Heaven with his gigantic white wings. Associated with Indra, King of Gods, as well as Surya, the Sun God, Uchchaishravas was a creature of great beauty and able to travel across the universe faster than the speed of thought.

There are various stories about the origin of Uchchaishravas. According to the text called Hariharachaturanga, *this divine horse emerged from a sacrificial fire held by Brahma, the Creator of the Universe. Yet another tale describes Uchchaishravas as a form of Krishna born of the* amrita, *or nectar of immortality in the Ocean of Milk.*

Throughout history, the appearance of white horses was considered to be prophetic as they were the mounts of great warriors who saved the universe from destruction. Vishnu's last and tenth avatar, who is yet to appear on earth, is that of Kalki, the fierce warrior. It is believed that Kalki will appear on a white horse resembling Uchchaishravas and bring about the destruction of all evil in the kaliyuga, *or age of darkness and destruction.*

Read Uchchaishravas's story as he whizzes across Heaven and earth on exciting adventures and grand quests . . .

CHAPTER ONE

A WHITE HORSE AND THE FOAMING SEA

Many, many things have threatened to destroy the balance between good and evil in the universe including wicked demons, terrible curses, foolish mistakes and ego clashes between gods. However, once the gods came very, very close to losing everything because of a garland.

The sage Durvasa was known to have a quick temper. Once he flew into a fit of rage when a garland he had offered to Airavata, Indra's elephant, was carelessly tossed away as it was attracting bees and plaguing poor Airavata. Furious at the insult to the garland, which should have been respected as *prasad*, or a blessing from the venerated sage, Durvasa was most displeased at the gods in general and cursed them aloud. As a result of Durvasa's curse, all the gods lost their immortality. Immediately, there was pandemonium as the gods feared that the *asuras* would have complete control over Heaven without the gods' immortality to protect them from the evil weapons.

Thereafter, the other sages went to Durvasa, begging him to reconsider his decision, as evil would reign supreme in a world where gods could die. Finally Durvasa relented and told the gods that there was one way that they could regain their powers. Although, it was terribly difficult and would take hundreds of years to achieve, it could be done. 'You have to undertake the great *samudra manthan*, or the churning of the Ocean of Milk,' said Durvasa. 'For deep within it lies the fabled *amrita* which will help you regain your powers again. Now do not think for a moment

that it will be easy. You will need the help of the demons and face great perils in order to get the *amrita*. But if you are persistent enough, it will be yours and the curse will be undone,' concluded the great sage, raising his hand to bless them.

The gods looked at each other in great confusion. They knew that the great ocean was a mighty place and the gods couldn't possibly churn it on their own. So Vishnu, the Preserver of the Universe, came forward and advised the gods to take the help of the *asuras*. 'Offer

them a share,' he suggested, and when the gods seemed reluctant about this, he added, 'and then we will see what happens.'

So for a while, a temporary truce was declared between the gods and the demons as they set about churning the ocean. Both parties knew that this was a really difficult task which would take a long, long time. The mountain Mandara was used as a churning rod and the powerful snake Vasuki agreed to let himself be used as the rope for churning. The *devas* held Vasuki's tail and the *asuras* took hold of his head. As the churning commenced, the mountain Mandara began to sink in the ocean.

The gods once again began despairing, and seeing their plight, Lord Vishnu came to the rescue. He took on the form of *kurma*, or the tortoise, and held the mountain steady on his hard, stone-like back and the churning resumed.

However, this was not the end of the troubles. In due course, Vasuki, being pulled on every side, felt a great discomfort and threw up a terrible dark poison called Halahala that made the ocean waters spew noxious fumes. As the air itself turned poisonous, the gods and *asuras* retreated to the banks and abandoned the churning.

This time, it was the all-powerful Lord Shiva, who appeared to save the day. He cupped the poison in his palms and swallowed it. The Goddess Parvati clasped him gently by the throat so that the poison would stay there and not move further down. Although his throat turned blue, Shiva remained unharmed. He is therefore known as Nilakantha, or the blue-throated one.

After many years had elapsed, Varuni, the Goddess of Wine, emerged from the ocean. She was followed by the Parijat, a tree so exquisite that it came to occupy the place of pride in Indra's famed garden in Heaven. A jewel named Kaustubha then came forth and Lord Vishnu accepted it as his adornment. It was the turn of three wonderful animals to emerge next. The first was Kapila the cow, the second was Airavata the elephant, who had regained his lost lustre, and finally emerged the magnificent white horse, Uchchaishravas.

Uchchaishravas broke through the frothy white waters and galloped across the ocean bed. His beauty was so stunning, his body so graceful, that all those who were present, stopped what they were doing to stare at this glorious creature. Many other wondrous creatures came after Uchchaishravas, until it was the turn of Dhanvantari, the Physician of the Gods, who emerged with a pot of *amrita* held secure in his hands.

Lord Vishnu could foresee the harm that could befall if the *asuras* became immortal, so he took on the form of a gorgeous woman called Mohini. So charmed were the *asuras* that, when she offered to serve the *amrita* to them, they willingly handed over their share.

However, the moment she got hold of the nectar of immortality, she whisked it away to the gods and served it to them instead. Thus, the gods once again became immortal and more powerful than the demons, for now they could never be killed. They defeated the demons and regained Heaven.

Meanwhile, Uchchaishravas was galloping along the banks of the Ocean of Milk with his wild mane flying out and his seven heads moving in unison. He was a truly divine creature, touched by the *amrita* and a thing of eternal beauty. The moment Indra saw him, he was entranced and claimed this heavenly horse for himself. Thus, the seven-headed Uchchaishravas made his way to Heaven with the King of Gods. The deep connection between Indra and Uchchaishravas is apparent as the great horse accompanied Indra on several battles and in fact, his seven heads are also connected to Indra's powers.

Apart from being a sacred number associated with sages and gods, the number seven has great significance for Lord Indra. The god was believed to be a terrifying adversary of seven enemies, who could strike from seven directions. And so Uchchaishravas was born with seven heads and these were turned in the direction of the seven deadly enemies.

CHAPTER TWO

A CRUEL BET BETWEEN SISTERS

However, before Uchchaishravas made his way to Heaven with Indra, something happened which ended all ties between two sisters who had once been as close as peas in a pod.

The sage Kashyapa had many wives, two of whom were sisters who had been inseparable in their childhood—Kadru and Vinata. Blessed by the gods, each of them gave birth to a powerful race of creatures. Kadru became the mother of all the snakes in the world whereas Vinata was blessed with two demigods—Aruna and Garuda.

Although, they had once been close, ever since they had been married to the same man, they had grown apart. Kadru was extremely jealous of her gentler sister and kept trying to hatch vicious plots against her. Now both Vinata and Kadru knew about the *samudra manthan*, or the churning of the ocean. They would go to the Ocean of Milk from time to time to see what it yielded.

One morning, as the two sisters looked on and the foam rose high from the ocean below them, they saw Uchchaishravas emerge from the waves. He was one of three precious animals that came forth from the churning. Both sisters looked on mesmerized at his beauty as they had never seen a creature so dazzlingly white.

'It is such a gorgeous animal. I have never seen anything like it,' gushed Vinata.

'Indeed,' said Kadru, who could rarely bring herself to agree with Vinata. She looked over the horse searching for a fault, but could find none. At that very moment, a clever plan began to form in her mind. 'Do you really think it's all white?' she asked with a strange expression on her face.

Vinata nodded with certainty. She couldn't take her eyes off the magnificent Uchchaishravas. 'It is white as white can ever be: whiter than the ocean foam, whiter than even Airavata's tusks and whiter than the purest milk,' she said still gazing at the magnificent horse.

'Well, I think you are mistaken and it is jet-black in colour. Blacker than night and blacker than the darkest hair on your head,' countered Kadru.

Vinata peered below to make sure, and shook her head in disbelief. 'Everything about it is white, sister.'

'Oh is that so? Then let's bet on it, shall we?' taunted Kadru. She was trying to egg on Vinata, hoping she would fall to her bait. Vinata laughed carelessly, 'A bet, sister? Are you sure? Because you are going to lose.'

'We'll see,' said Kadru mockingly. 'I say it is black. And you say it is white. So, whoever loses shall be the other one's slave for now and evermore. Do you agree?'

Vinata nodded. She couldn't possibly imagine herself losing the bet, nor did she think her sister, should she win, would actually make her a slave.

Kadru turned away then. She summoned all her children to her, in the way she had many times before. And sure enough, all the snakes of the world, in their thousands and millions, came wriggling through the skies, swimming across all the oceans of the universe to answer their mother's call.

'What is it, mother? Why have you called us?'

Kadru lowered her voice and told them what it was she wanted them to do.

'You must make your way to that fine horse gambolling in the ocean over there. He is huge and fierce but you mustn't be scared. For your mother's sake, you must wriggle up to him and cover his body, till every square inch of white looks black. Now go and do that at once.'

When some of the snakes hesitated, for not all snakes were evil, Kadru cursed them, saying they would all be destroyed one day in a fire. Alarmed at this threat, most snakes did as their mother commanded. They crawled up to Uchchaishravas as he galloped through the waves and clambered all over him, until not a speck of white was visible on his body.

Now Uchchaishravas was mildly surprised to see all the snakes crawling all over him. However, he knew he was very powerful and they could do little to harm him. And so he ran even faster to shake these creatures off. As he ran, Kadru pointed him out to her sister.

'There he goes, sister. Your magnificent white horse! Do you still think he is white as milk?'

And as Vinata looked, she saw to her horror that Kadru had indeed been right. No longer was it a white horse standing before her but one that was jet-black in colour, darker than the night sky itself.

She abjectly accepted her defeat knowing that she had been tricked. Kadru ordered Vinata to proceed to the netherworld where she would serve her and her many snake children for all of eternity.

Soon after Vinata made her way to the netherworld, the snakes slipped off Uchchaishravas and slid away silently. And Uchchaishravas, rid of his fake black skin, was back to being a glorious shade of white again.

CHAPTER THREE

GODDESS LAKSHMI'S WONDERFUL GIFTS

Most divine creatures in the universe have several origin stories and Uchchaishravas is no different. According to one such tale, Uchchaishravas did not belong to Indra and instead was a creature of the *asura* king Bali.

It is believed that Lakshmi, the Goddess of Wealth, also emerged from the churning of the ocean along with all the treasures hidden deep within it. As she came out of the foamy waters, she was accompanied by a number of wonderful creatures and magical objects. These included the many-tusked white elephant called

Airavata and the snow-white, seven-headed flying horse called Uchchaishravas. Along with them emerged a number of treasures like a golden crown embedded with precious jewels, an embroidered footstool, a parasol made of the finest silk in the universe, a fly-whisk that spread divine fragrance every time it was swatted, a fan made of rare bird feathers, a conch-shell and a magnificent bow.

As the gods and the demons continued churning, the ocean roared, the snake-king Vasuki hissed and the harsh breathing of the gods and the *asuras* filled the

skies. But, the moment Goddess Lakshmi emerged from the waters, all at once, a silence fell all around. Everyone looked agape at the wondrous goddess who had emerged from the ocean and moments later, her voice rang clearly out across the entire universe.

Gesturing towards the objects she had around her, she said, 'These things around me all represent kingship. They should rightly go to someone who is deserving of these magical things and the power they bestow on the owner. The person who wishes to possess these symbols I have around me must prove he is worthy and that these will be used to forever protect, shelter and help all that has life and needs help.'

As Lakshmi spoke, both Uchchaishravas and Airavata stood as magnificent sentinels on either side of her, adding grandeur to the already resplendent goddess.

Lakshmi had barely finished speaking when Indra, the King of Gods and the Lord of Heaven, spoke up. Now Indra was a very proud god who was extremely sure of himself and his powers. He bowed to the goddess and began his speech. 'O Goddess of Wealth, I think I am the one king truly deserving of these symbols and magnificent creatures. I am the King of Gods and Lord of Heaven. All the other gods including the great Agni, Vayu and Varuna defer to me. Why, even the mighty Sun God, Surya withdraws when I decide to create rain on earth.'

Lakshmi heard him out and then shook her head and responded, 'Lord Indra, I know you are a great god and one of the most magnificent kings in all the three worlds. Yet, there is one fatal flaw you possess and that makes you unworthy of these divine symbols.' All those present looked surprised including Indra and waited for the goddess to explain further.

'You are too fond of pleasure,' Goddess Lakshmi continued. 'There have been days and nights that you have been locked in your palace eating good food, drinking and watching the *apsaras* dance, while outside the *asuras* grew in strength and spread terror everywhere. That is not the sign of a good king.'

Indra blushed and withdrew in considerable embarrassment.

The next contender was Bali, the great *asura* king. He stood up towering over the others who were present and said, 'I am far stronger than Indra can ever be. In a short time, I have expanded my realm in every direction. I already have more riches than I wish to possess, but I do assure you, O Goddess of Light and Prosperity, that the symbols you hold, are those I would cherish greatly and uphold to the best of my ability and power.'

However, Bali's earnest appeal did little to move Lakshmi. Once again she shook her head decisively and responded, 'No, even you are not deserving of these, great though you may be. You have immense wealth and are still not satisfied. There is no limit to your desire for power, though you may be generous to a fault. Power has made you arrogant and even your desire to help and donate is tinged by it.'

Bali too hung his head and withdrew. Now Lakshmi knew who would be ideal for the symbols she held. It would have to be a king who was stable and not crazy about the short-lived pursuits of wealth, power and pleasure. He had to be someone everyone on Heaven

and earth could trust. He would be someone who would judge wisely and well, conduct himself virtuously and use his power for the good of everyone.

Only one god fulfilled all these criteria—Lord Vishnu, the Preserver of the Universe. And thus Lakshmi, the Goddess of Wealth, Light and Prosperity, chose Lord Vishnu as her consort, and along with all the wealth that emerged with her from the ocean, made her way to his fabled abode, Vaikuntha.

Now while the case of the magical gifts was easily decided, the wonderful animals were more difficult to give away as Airavata and Uchchaishravas were truly remarkable creatures and any king who owned them would increase in power and grandeur. Lord Vishnu already had a loyal retinue that chiefly comprised Garuda, the great devourer of snakes and Sheshanaga, the endless serpent.

In the end, after some debate, Airavata, the elephant, was claimed by Indra, for he had rain-giving powers too and Uchchaishravas, the snow-white, fleet-footed and seven-headed horse, went to the *asura* king, Bali.

But in an ironic and uncharacteristic twist, it was the god Indra who remained covetous of something which belonged to an *asura*. While Indra had immeasurable quantities of wealth and wonderful creatures in his stables, he still could not rest until he had the magnificent Uchchaishravas as well and he eventually defeated the *asura* and took Bali's magnificent horse for himself.

In most other versions of the story, this event is usually retold the other way round and Bali is always the one who seizes Uchchaishravas from his rightful owner—Lord Indra.

CHAPTER FOUR

BALI'S GENEROSITY

Now Uchchaishravas's dazzling beauty made him much coveted among the gods, especially Indra who treasured him greatly. The gods, after drinking the *amrita*, were restored to their former powers and regained Heaven. However, this was not the end of the trouble.

Not too long after the temporary truce of the *samundra manthan*, the enmity resumed between the *asuras* and the gods. Despite regaining their immortality, the gods lost Heaven yet again when faced with the formidable *asura* king Bali. Bali was the all-powerful grandson of Prahlada, the great demon king. A devout worshipper of Brahma, Bali had earned many magnificent gifts through his devotion. Armed with all his weapons and boons, he marched to the skies and conquered Heaven. As the new Lord of Heaven, he became master of all of Indra's possessions including the divine Uchchaishravas, who became his personal *vahana,* or vehicle. Riding the white horse, the demon king ruled over his newly acquired world with great pride.

The gods, ashamed by their defeat, retreated deep into the forests. Some of them went in search of Lord Vishnu, in his fabled home at Vaikuntha. Traumatized by their humiliating defeat, everywhere they went, they could hear the sound of Bali riding triumphantly on Uchchaishravas.

As he rode on the all-powerful Uchchaishravas, Bali was now unstoppable and made even more daring conquests across the universe.

The gods wishing to regain Heaven pleaded with Lord Vishnu to save them again. Bali had become too powerful to oppose and the gods feared they would soon have nowhere to hide. Lord Vishnu assured them that he would help them. Despite being an *asura*, Bali was a benevolent king. But on no count could an *asura* become more powerful than a god. And that was why the time had come for Lord Vishnu to intervene. He assumed the form of a dwarf called Vamana and turned up in Bali's kingdom as he performed a *yagna*, or holy sacrifice. Bali was known for his generosity and Vishnu knew he would not turn him down.

Joining the line of holy men in search of alms, Vamana disguised himself well. When his turn came, the dwarf asked for three paces of land. When a surprised Bali agreed, Vamana swelled up in size. Then with his first step he covered earth. With the second, he spanned Heaven. As he was about to take another step, he ran out of land to cover.

Now Bali had promised the dwarf land enough for three steps. And since Vamana had already covered the two worlds with his two steps, Bali offered his head to be kept under Vamana's foot to compensate for the third step. Vishnu as Vamana put a giant foot on the demon king's head and pushed him down to the underworld.

Bali was crushed, and the *devas* heaved a sigh of relief. Heaven was restored to the gods and Uchchaishravas was restored to Indra.

CHAPTER FIVE

INDRA'S FOLLY

Now everyone envied Indra as he owned the grandest and most beautiful of all horses, Uchchaishravas. And although Indra loved Uchchaishravas and was a wise and compassionate god who ruled his world well, he had a weakness for white horses. It was this shortcoming that led him to commit a great folly and anger a king. This in turn angered a sage and brought about great tragedy in the human world.

Once while King Sagara was performing his *ashwamedha yagna*, or the great horse sacrifice, Indra was close by. He caught a glimpse of the lovely white steed which was the sacrificial horse and immediately fell in love with the lovely creature. It is hard to believe that the Lord of Heaven would need to do this, but unable to resist its charm, he stole this handsome creature to add to his menagerie of white animals including Airavata and Uchchaishravas.

Now having the *yagna* disrupted, and the sacrificial steed stolen, was a great insult to the king and a bad omen for the kingdom. So Sagara sent his one thousand sons to search for the missing white horse. While on their mission, Sagara's sons found themselves in sage

Kapila's *ashrama*. The sage and his disciples were then in the midst of a prayer. As one thousand princes entered the *ashrama* on horseback, there was great commotion and the sages had to break their meditation. Kapila opened his eyes in rage and his fiery glare reduced Sagara's sons to ashes.

When, beseeched by their family to free their souls, Kapila prophesied that only if the Goddess Ganga could be persuaded to flow down to earth from Heaven, would the princes attain salvation. This was a near impossible task and it was only many hundreds of years later that a great-great-grandson of Sagara, called Bhagiratha, managed to secure Ganga's descent from Heaven and free the souls of Sagara's sons. And all of this happened because of one white horse!

Although Indra did feel a bit guilty at having caused all this mayhem, he was still not cured of his weakness for horses. He stole another spectacular sacrificial horse. This time, it was King Prithu who was the target of Indra's mischief. The King of Heaven disguised himself as a sage in ochre-coloured robes because no one would dare stop a holy man from entering the sacred area where the *yagna* was being conducted. Thereafter, he spirited the horse away. However, this time Lord Indra had to return the horse as Prithu's son saw him running away with it and gave chase.

Once he caught up with him, he confronted the god and said, 'You already have Uchchaishravas, the most splendid of horses. Why do you need to disrupt my father's sacrifice?'

Indra did not answer; instead, he prodded the horse into a gallop and was soon on the road to Heaven. The prince gave chase, and Indra was surprised at how quickly he gained speed and caught up with him. He

thought ruefully that Uchchaishravas would have taken him to Heaven in no time. He soon heard a shout from behind, 'O King of Gods, if you won't return the horse, I will be forced to challenge you to a duel.'

He was very near Heaven and knew that once the gods would see him with the stolen horse, they would realize he had done a wrong thing and force him to make amends. He also knew that Prithu was a human avatar of Lord Vishnu, and he could not afford a battle with a god more powerful than he was. Not only did he return the horse, he showered the young prince with lavish gifts before he returned home. Once back in Heaven, the first thing Lord Indra did was to go and see Uchchaishravas trotting in the heavenly pastures, as white as a magnificent cloud in the sky. As he looked at Uchchaishravas, he realized that no horse in the world could match up to his very own divine flying horse.

CHAPTER SIX

A THEFT AND A CURSE

Uchchaishravas, the foremost of all horses, was a symbol of Indra's glory and Indra was extremely proud as well as possessive about his wonderful creature. Anyone who eyed Uchchaishravas was usually punished or subject to great misfortune.

Once, the demon Tarakusara spotted Uchchaishravas in the sky and was immediately enamoured of his beauty. He sneaked into Heaven and robbed the divine horse from Indra's celestial abode. This was a very daring thing to do as the demon had crossed paths with the King of Gods himself.

But that was because Tarakasura was no ordinary demon. Blessed by Brahma, the Creator of the Universe, with near immortality, he was as powerful as the gods themselves. The only being who could kill Tarakasura would have to be a son of Lord Shiva. Tarakasura had thought he was being very clever in asking for such a boon, as Shiva at that time had just lost his wife Sati, and had no intention of marrying again.

However, many years later, he met Parvati and pleased with her devotion and penances he married her. Soon enough, they were blessed with a son—Kartikeya.

Now Tarakasura, knowing the flaw in the boon granted by Brahma, began to fear for his life. He looked for Kartikeya long and hard, but it was in vain, for Nandi, Shiva's *vahana*, had spirited him away to Mount Kailash. When the time came to battle Tarakasura, Kartikeya rode out to battle on a peacock. He killed Tarakasura, ended the menace and once again Uchchaishravas was restored to Indra and the gods.

Thus all those who coveted Uchchaishravas

wrongly usually met with a bad end. And this was the case whether they were gods or *asuras*.

And indeed Uchchaishravas's beauty was such that even the gods could rarely resist his charms and there are various stories about divine beings who were punished because of this reason.

One such story is that of Lord Revanta who was the God of Hunting and Protector of Forests, Goddess Parvati and Uchchaishravas. Revanta, was the son of Surya, the Sun God, and Sanjana, daughter of Vishvakarma, the Universal Architect.

Now although Sanjana was married to Surya, she was unable to bear his radiance for too long. So, she retreated to the forests, taking on the form of a mare, and she placed her shadow—Chhaya, who was her lookalike in every way—in her place as Surya's wife.

When Surya came to know in course of time that Chhaya was not the real Sanjana, he looked for her everywhere. Finally, he found her in the forests of Uttarkuru. Since she was now a mare, Surya approached her disguised as a horse in turn and they lived happily in their equine forms and even had three children—the Ashwin twins and Revanta.

One day, Revanta borrowed Uchchaishravas from Lord Indra and went out riding. He came to Vaikuntha on Uchchaishravas. At the very sight of the splendid horse, Lakshmi, Lord Vishnu's consort was completely mesmerized and desired him greatly. So spellbound was she by Uchchaishravas's beauty that she did not hear the question addressed to her by Lord Vishnu.

Annoyed by the inattention and suspecting that Lakshmi coveted Uchchaishravas, he cursed her. 'Do you not know my power?' said Lord Vishnu, irritated at his wife's absent-mindedness. 'Men, demons and gods pay obeisance to me and yet you, my consort and my very own wife, choose to ignore me when I speak. Were you so busy looking at Uchchaishravas's great beauty that you could not even hear my question? For this dishonour to me, I curse you. As you ignored me for a horse, so in one of your many incarnations, O great goddess, you shall be born a mare.'

And thus all those who eyed Uchchaishravas wrongly, were punished in some form or the other, even if they were the gods themselves. Such was the divinity and power of this celestial horse, and the possessiveness that Indra displayed towards him.

CHAPTER SEVEN

A CASE OF STOLEN EARRINGS

Takshak, the snake-king, was one of the children of Kadru, who was known for his mischievous and wicked ways. Once, he stole the earrings which the sage called Uttanka had got for his guru's wife and it took all of Indra's wiles to retrieve them; for Uttanka was a great devotee of Lord Indra and had asked the god for his help.

This incident took place when Uttanka was still a youth and had just completed his studies under his guru, the great sage Gautama. Now the time had come for him to offer *guru dakshina*, or an offering a student makes to his teacher as an expression of gratitude. His guru wanted to please his wife. And sage Gautama's wife was very fond of earrings. So, as per his guru's wishes, Uttanka set about getting a pair of very special earrings made for her by renowned artisans in a faraway land. They were very precious and worth a small fortune.

After getting the earrings, he began his journey homewards. On the way, he felt very thirsty and stopped to drink water from a nearby stream. He left his belongings by a bush as he knelt on the riverbank to drink water.

A beggar, who had been following him for a while, took this chance and quickly stole the bundle containing the precious earrings.

Uttanka happened to see this and ran after him. When the beggar was unable to throw him off, he changed into his true shape. And Uttanka realized that it was no other than Takshak, that most wicked and mischievous of serpents. Before Uttanka could catch up with him, Takshak dropped to the ground and wriggled away instantly into a dark hole that opened up in front of him.

Uttanka tried his best to dig open the hole, first with his fingers and then with a stick, but he failed to make any progress. Finally, fearing the wrath of his guru at having failed the task that had been set for him, he turned to Indra, the King of Gods, to intervene in the matter. Indra took pity on this young sage who was one of his great devotees and tore the hole open with his powerful weapon—the Vajra.

Almost immediately Uttanka stepped into the darkness and found himself in Nagaloka, or the kingdom of the serpents. He was amazed to see a most wonderful city inside, with sparkling palaces and

gems that lit up the whole place. Uttanka, who was by now desperate to reclaim his earrings, knew that he could not fight these powerful *nagas*, or snakes. So, he decided to impress them instead. Uttanka was a great poet and could charm anyone with his lovely words. He composed the most beautiful verses praising the snakes and their underground home right on the spot and recited them aloud.

For all his efforts though, he got a spellbound audience, but there was no trace of the earrings or Takshak. Uttanka wandered around the city of the snakes, desperate to find the snake-king but he had simply and very literally vanished into the ground. Once again he prayed to Indra, asking for his help.

Indra, hearing his prayers, appeared before him yet again. This time he was mounted on his divine horse Uchchaishravas. He said to Uttanka, 'Blow into Uchchaishravas's ear and in no time your deed shall be done.'

Heeding Indra's advice, Uttanka raised himself on his toes and blew hard into the ear of the horse. At once, towering golden flames began emerging from the divine horse's nostrils. Soon, there was thick smoke all around and the magnificent kingdom of the serpents was engulfed in deadly fumes which made everyone breathless. All the snakes began fainting with the heat. Finally, unable to bear the choking smoke, Takshak also emerged from his hiding place.

He begged Uchchaishravas for mercy as he writhed in agony. Finally, at a word from Uttanka, Uchchaishravas quietened down and the fire and smoke cleared up.

Takshak immediately restored the earrings to Uttanka, who in turn thanked Indra profusely. The Lord of Heaven patted his wonderful companion and galloped away to Heaven, leaving a relieved devotee and chastised snake in his wake.

CHAPTER EIGHT

LORD VISHNU'S HORSE AVATARS

It is believed that one of the reasons for Uchchaishravas's greatness and powers is the fact that he is believed to be an avatar of Krishna, or the powerful Lord Vishnu himself. This fact is also proven by Lord Vishnu's fondness and affinity for all horses.

When Vishnu incarnated as Rama to kill the evil *rakshasa*, Ravana, his kingdom Ayodhya was reputed to be the most splendid of all cities. The city was protected by a huge contingent of brave warriors who were skilled in every art of warfare. And these warriors rode the finest

of horses in the kingdom, procured from countries far and wide and they were all milk-white, just like the king of horses, Uchchaishravas.

The white horse was regarded as the universal saviour and Lord Vishnu had himself assumed the form of a half-man half-horse called Hayagriva.

Once there was a demon named Hayagriva who was the son of the great sage Kashyapa. Hayagriva was a great devotee of Goddess Durga and pleased her with his penances. She blessed him saying that from now he was near immortal as he could only be killed by another Hayagriva. Armed with such a boon, Hayagriva considered himself invincible and began harassing the gods.

The troubled gods appealed to Lord Vishnu to help them. And although the great Preserver of the Universe fought a long and hard battle, he was still unable to kill the demon Hayagriva because he was protected by Goddess Durga's blessing.

Tired and exhausted after the battle, Lord Vishnu returned to his resting place at Vaikuntha to recuperate. As he lay in a yogic posture, his head supported by the upper end of his tautly strung bow, the gods again arrived, asking for help against Hayagriva's atrocities. But despite their clamour, they were unable to rouse him from his pensive mood.

Left with no option, the gods then asked a swarm of termites to wake Vishnu up by gnawing away the string of the bow on which his head rested. As the termites nibbled away, the string broke with a loud, resounding twang that made the entire universe tremble. The broken string ricocheted with such force that Lord Vishnu's head was forcibly severed from his body.

The contingent of shocked gods froze in horror. Utterly horrified by what they had done, they realized that only the Goddess Durga could help them. They prayed to her till she appeared before them. Appeased by their prayers, she reassured the gods: 'You need not fear,' she told them. 'There is no incident in this universe that is without purpose.'

She then told the gods of the boon she had granted the demon Hayagriva, which made him near impossible

to kill. 'However, there is a way to end his life,' she said. 'Attach the head of a horse to Lord Vishnu's neck so that he becomes a Hayagriva—a half-man and half-horse. Once that is done, he will be able to defeat the demon and save the universe.'

It was Lord Brahma who attached the head of a white horse to Vishnu. The god immediately revived and entered into a fierce duel with Hayagriva. After a short battle, Vishnu took off the demon's head and restored peace to the world of the *devas*.

Lord Vishnu's Hayagriva avatar, is another divine horse, second only to Uchchaishravas, the great king of horses who was also the first horse in the world.

MythNotes

Uchchaishravas has been associated with several gods and divinities apart from Indra. In some texts, Surya, or the Sun God, is also called Tarkshya and he appears as a radiant winged horse. Lord Vayu, the Wind God, had a thousand white or purple horses pulling his chariot as he flew across the universe with his life-giving winds. Surya was also believed to drive through Heaven in his triumphal chariot harnessed by seven horses or one horse with seven heads, which represent the seven colours of the rainbow. His charioteer was Aruna, the brother of Garuda, the great bird-king.

The wonderful myths of this divine flying horse have led to his adaptation in popular culture and George Harrison's music label, Dark Horse Records, has a logo inspired by the great Uchchaishravas.

In Sanskrit, the term Uchchaishravas means 'long ears' and 'neighing aloud' which points to the origin of the term 'ashwa' meaning horse.

According to the Puranas, horses originated on earth after Lord Indra severed the wings of Uchchaishravas and sent him to earth. His wings were cut off so that he could not fly back to Heaven and would be restricted to earth. Thus Uchchaishravas stayed on earth to father the race of horses, which in turn would help mankind face great battles and travel vast distances across the land.